THE WEEK THAT LED TO EASTER

The Story of Holy Week Matthew 21:1–28:10; Mark 11:1–16:8; Luke 19:29–24:12; and John 12:12–20:10 for children

Written by Joanne Larrison ∅ Illustrated by Jenny Williams

Arch® Books
Copyright © 2001 Concordia Publishing House
3558 S. Jefferson Avenue, St. Louis, MO 63118-3968
Printed in Columbia

All rights reserved. No part of this publication may be reproduced, stored in a retrieval system, or transmitted, in any form or by any means, electronic, mechanical, photocopying, recording, or otherwise, without the prior written permission of Concordia Publishing House.

"Hosanna! Sing to Christ the King,"
Crowds shouted as He came.
They had heard the many stories—
How He healed the sick and lame.

Jerusalem was crowded.
The Passover had begun—
A time to remember Egypt,
And to have a little fun.

The 12 disciples led the way
To the upper room
Where Jesus shared His final meal—
He knew His life was doomed.

He told them that His life would end,
And that He'd be betrayed.
He shared His bread and wine with them,
Then bowed His head and prayed.

Jesus asked to be remembered
For the sins He'd take away.
He told them of God's final plan.
And that He could not stay.

Then He prayed to God to guide Him—
To give strength along the way.
For He understood the suff'ring
And the price that He must pay.

The leaders and guards were waiting
To take Him away from town.
They would nail Him to a wooden cross,
Place on His head a thorny crown.

They had turned the crowd against Him,
Said, "He's *not* God's Son to fear."
And the crowd yelled, "CRUCIFY Him!"
Jesus did not shed a tear.

The sky turned black and thunder rolled.
Jesus said His final words:
"Please forgive them, Father."
"It is finished!" they then heard.

Friends sealed Him in a cold, dark cave
With a big stone for a door.
Not many came to see Him,
For the crowds—they cared no more.

Though God's plan now seemed completed
To the people here on earth,
Christ's death was just the beginning—
A new chance for our rebirth.

For when Jesus died, He died to save
All people great and small.
He took our sins away from us—
T'was the greatest gift of all.

He rose again on Easter day.
The people were amazed,
For God's plan now was understood.
They gave their love and praise.

Jesus is *still* alive today.
He reigns in heaven above.
He forgives us and He guides us,
And fills our hearts with love.

Dear Parents:

The week that led to Easter is significant in the lives of Christians. It is a sober time, tracing the steps of Christ to the cross. Yet it leads to jubilant celebration as Christ defeats Satan and sin, opening the door of heaven to all believers.

The week that led to Easter is called "Holy Week," and it is indeed holy. It frames the New Testament fulfillment of God's Old Testament promise to send a Savior. It is a week worth commemorating.

Set aside time as a family to review what happened during Holy Week. Check out the Bible references on page 1, and decide which to use. Read a portion of the Passion story each day from Palm Sunday to Easter. After each reading, ask your children to retell that portion of the story using their own words. Raid your closets for suitable props and costumes. Act out the story, trying to include all the characters—even the crowd that yells, "Crucify Him!" In so doing, the week that led to Easter will take on new meaning and be holy indeed.

The Editor